GINGER'S
Story

A Golden Retriever Reflects
Upon Her Life With Humans

Steven M. Wells

Medina, Washington

*Ann,
Enjoy the story-
Steve*

ISBN-10: 1456329383
EAN-13: 9781456329389

For my daughter Gabrielle,
who teaches me the meaning of love each day.

A New Day

As I went outside late in the morning I noticed the air felt cool and slightly damp. From my limited experience I knew that the afternoon sun would soon burn through the thin layer of clouds and bring warmth. I gazed at the acre-sized lawn, mowed earlier in the morning, and took in its powerful fragrance of freshly cut grass. In the center of the lawn and away from the owner's home a stainless steel portable pen, about eight feet square, had been erected earlier that day and ample room remained for guests to arrive and park their cars.

My litter mates and I had just finished our baths and our coats had been blown dry to a silky smooth texture. We were golden retriever puppies, and our litter included three males and four females. On this day prospective owners would come to meet us. My name is Ginger and this is my story.

Once grooming was complete, our breeder tied colored pieces of ribbon around our necks. Each dog wore a unique color. I was Orange Girl. My sisters were Purple Girl, Black Girl, and Red Girl. The boys were Brown Boy, Blue Boy, and Green Boy. Our future owners would later give us formal names.

This exciting event of introducing puppies to owners was as important to us as it was to the new owner. As the breeder accepted orders for us she assigned each owner a pick number. The first order accepted was assigned first pick, the second one second pick and so on. On this day owners would meet the puppies and choose their favorites, much like children might do in a sandlot baseball game. Then over the next several weeks they would exercise their picks. Earlier pick numbers were more likely to give owners their first choice.

Some owners preferred females while others wanted males. Some preferred puppies with aggressive traits, such as inquisitive or active, while others wanted puppies with more sedate personalities. It was important for happiness at home that each puppy was well matched with the new owner's personality and interests. Our breeder helped in this process since she had observed us from birth six weeks earlier. She would size up the personality of the new owner and make suggestions about which of us would be well suited for him or her.

Our breeder was among the best in the state. She requested of each owner a signed contract with a number of provisions: the owner would provide a fenced yard, take the puppy to an obedience class, and most importantly, if for any reason the owner decided he or she could no longer care for the dog at any age, the puppy would be returned to the breeder. It was very important to her that the owners must not sell us or give us away to anyone else. This was for our protection, and our breeder wanted assurance that we would always remain in good hands. She genuinely cared for each and every puppy she placed with new owners.

We had been in the shiny steel pen for a short period of time when I heard the crunching of tires on gravel signaling the arrival of the first car. A couple with a young boy got out and walked over near our pen where the breeder was waiting. In no time at all other cars came up the drive until there were a total of seven. The future owners were soon milling about talking with each other and our breeder.

The event formally began with a review of the care a puppy needs during its first few weeks at home. This was followed by a quick reminder of the terms in the purchase agreement. Lastly there was a demonstration with Blue Boy on how to trim sharp puppy toenails with a small motorized grinding tool. It involved placing a small dab of peanut butter in the roof of the puppy's mouth to distract it while the breeder ground off the sharp points of the nails. I love peanut butter and it worked with me every time. I was usually so busy trying to lick peanut butter off of the roof of my mouth that I completely forgot about the grinding noise down by my paws.

Soon it was time to meet the owners. We were all very excited. Some of my sisters were still lying motionless on the grass while the boys were roaming around, clumsily stepping and tripping over everything in their way. For reasons I never understood, Brown Boy often chewed on my ears, which annoyed me. I'd yelp, and he'd stop, but only for a while. What was it about my ears he found so interesting?

I was carefully eyeing the owners wondering if any of them would want me. I noticed one little boy being very rough with Black Girl. I didn't like that. A woman in a pink sweater picked up Brown Boy and started kissing him and telling him how cute he was. I thought she probably wouldn't say that if he started chewing on her ears with those needle sharp teeth of his.

I then noticed a tall girl with long brown hair in a ponytail standing close to her father's leg. She seemed timid and hesitated to go near the pen. Her father encouraged her and gently moved her closer. She observed the five of us remaining in the pen and looked straight at me. I opened up my brown eyes as large as possible and tried to look alert. She moved in my direction, reached down in the pen, and gently picked me up. I could tell she was very cautious. I liked that. I wagged my tail a little. She walked over to an area of grass and gently put me down. I licked her hand and again looked at her with my brown eyes. She seemed to notice this and looked happy, although I could tell she was still hesitant. She gently rubbed my soft pink tummy and my floppy ears.

I listened carefully as her father walked over, sat down next to us, and said, "Gabrielle, do you like Orange Girl?"

Gabrielle said, "Yes, Dad, she's really cute, and I think she likes me!"

Her dad replied, "How can you tell she likes you?"

"Because she has big brown eyes and it feels like she is talking to me when she looks at me," Gabrielle said. "I want her!"

I liked Gabrielle, and after she put me back into the pen no other family picked me up. I felt this was a good sign. Maybe Gabrielle would receive her first and only pick.

The Lecture

The owners departed while the breeder and her husband returned the pen to the garage and put the table in the storage shed. My litter mates and I were placed back inside the house with our parents. I started wondering who my new owner would be.

Over the next two weeks, as we got bigger and stronger, our parents started our lessons, telling us what was expected of us as we went out into the world with our human owners. They explained how important our role was and some of the difficulties we should expect to encounter.

The biggest challenge, they explained, was our ability to understand what humans were saying while they could not understand us. It was important for humans to have a companion with whom they could talk and yet not experience conflict from what might be said in response. This explains why eye contact is so important for dogs to communicate. Eye contact, erectness, and the motion of our tails, position of our ears, and sounds such as barking and sighing, are all methods of communication we must master. The best owners will quickly learn to recognize these signals. Owners who are less sensitive will need more time to understand. And some will be oblivious. In the end our job is to make all of them feel loved.

Humans, they went on to explain, while capable of great intellectual achievements, were often emotionally immature. For some reason, while teachings of history, science, and math were all built upon increasing knowledge transferred among generations, when it came to emotional skills such as compassion, trust, and loyalty, humans appear reluctant to learn from the experiences of each preceding generation. Our role as dogs is to teach humans these necessary skills and bring healthy emotions into their lives.

They explained to us how a strong bond will develop between us and children if we are fortunate enough to be placed in a family with them. "While all human contact is important," they said, "children find their interaction with dogs extremely rewarding."

They mentioned research showing that 80 percent of children refer to themselves as a pet's mother or father, and that if given a choice, more than half of those children would prefer to be with a pet over a family member if stranded on a desert island. "Children relate to pets," they said, "and our time with them brings almost immeasurable happiness to their lives."

During the last lesson they told us that our lives were much shorter than humans. They explained that this important truth helps teach humans to accept loss, an emotional event they seem neither adept at nor interested in confronting. They concluded by telling us that only by experiencing attachment and accepting loss can humans fully embrace the fullness of their lives.

My New Home

As the day approached for owners to start picking up their new puppies, I became increasingly nervous. I was leaving little puddles all over our pen. I really wanted Gabrielle, the cute tall girl with the long brown hair, to pick me. I didn't know her father's pick order, so I just had to wait and see. The first puppy to get picked was Brown Boy. This didn't surprise me. He was seriously cute and cuddly even with his annoying ear chewing habit. The woman with the pink sweater from the first meeting was the first in pick order and away he went.

Next the family with the rather rough boy came and picked Black Girl. I hoped that his parents would take good care of her and make sure their son learned the proper way to care for puppies. We are very helpless while young puppies and need a lot of nurturing. I had to trust that the breeder knew what she was doing when she agreed to assign them a dog.

There were no additional pick-ups that day. I was happy that Gabrielle had not come to pick anyone else. But I didn't know what tomorrow would bring. I tried to remain hopeful.

The next morning after breakfast we played with some of our toys in the pen. I looked over when I heard the door to the house open. I watched as Gabrielle and her father walked in and stood by the door to our room. I looked into

Gabrielle's beautiful blue eyes as the breeder walked to the pen, leaned over, and picked me up and handed me to her. The smile on Gabrielle's face was broad and her eyes were bright with excitement. She had picked me. I felt I was the luckiest puppy in the world.

The breeder went over some forms and instructions with her father, named Steve, and asked for his signature while Gabrielle held me tight. When they were finished, she carried me out to the car and placed me in a white plastic clothes basket, the kind with a mesh of rectangular holes, which had a soft towel in the bottom. The basket was placed on the back seat of the car and Gabrielle climbed in next to me and firmly held onto the basket.

As Gabrielle's father drove I kept looking around the car observing everything. There were so many new smells. Dogs have one hundred times more powerful sensitivity to smells than humans due to their large nasal cavities and many more sensory cells. I tried to smell Gabrielle. It was a smell I wanted to remember forever. She looked at me often as she gently rubbed my head and body.

When we arrived at my new home, Gabrielle took me out to the back yard, which was fenced as required by the contract. It looked very large, and with my small size all I could see were several tall magnolia trees flanking a set of rock steps leading up to a terrace filled with rhododendrons. After I went to the bathroom, Gabrielle picked me up and took me inside the house to the laundry room where I was shown my new crate. This large rectangular cage made out of metal grating included a cushion in the bottom and a swinging door with a latch on front. This is where I would sleep for the next several months.

After my first dinner Steve asked Gabrielle, "What name are you going to give Orange Girl?"

Gabrielle said, "Dad, I've been thinking about that and I like the name Ginger. She has color like ginger, and that's one of my favorite names for a dog."

"Well then," Steve said, "I think Ginger is a great name."

Bad News

Over the next several weeks my life took on a rhythm of sleeping, eating, playing, and going outdoors. A young dog's skeletal system is not well developed, so walking on hard surfaces can be harmful and should be avoided. So when I got out of my cage to play, it was usually in the grass or on a carpeted floor in the house. At night when Gabrielle and her dad were asleep in their bedrooms and I had to go to the bathroom, I would whimper and cry, and within a few minutes Steve would come downstairs, unlock the crate then carefully pick me up and take me out to the back yard. He would put me down and often pull up a folding chair and wait for me to sniff around until I found the perfect place to relieve myself. He was always very patient, and I'm sure happy that it was summer so the late nights and early mornings were warm.

When I was twelve weeks old I was taken to a veterinary doctor for a checkup. The doctor looked at my eyes and my ears, checked my paws, felt my tummy, and placed a small, cold, metal disk called a stethoscope on my body and listened. He did this on either side of my chest. After doing this several times he left the room and returned with another stethoscope with a small box attached to it. He told Steve that it was an electronic stethoscope and more sensitive to sound. After listening again he frowned and explained he had heard a heart murmur and confirmed it with the more sensitive stethoscope. He went on to explain that such murmurs can be transitory and go away as puppies get older. He said he'd keep an eye on it and check it again when I was six months old.

I loved my time with Gabrielle. She was very gentle with me and frequently took me out to the grass in the front yard and brushed my fur with a puppy brush. I enjoyed the times I got to sleep on her bed. Sometimes at night when Steve had already gone to his bed she would sneak me upstairs and let me sleep with her. Other times for fun she would crawl into my crate with me and pretend she was a dog too. Gabrielle's mom and dad were divorced and she spent alternating weeks with each parent. The weeks she was gone I missed her and felt lonelier in my crate at night.

When I was six months old, I went back to the veterinarian. He rechecked my heart with the stethoscope and confirmed that he could still hear my murmur. He instructed Steve that it was important that I be seen by a canine cardiologist. He said there were only two in the state of Washington and gave him the name and phone number of the nearest one.

Three weeks later I went back to the veterinary office where I was examined by the cardiologist. He put a plastic wand near my heart that displayed images of my heart valves opening and closing on a nearby monitor. Throughout the day he examined a number of dogs, explaining the condition of each to my veterinarian, who at the end of the day summarized the findings for the owners.

When it was my turn to be picked up, my veterinarian and I went to the examination room where Steve was waiting. He asked, "What did the cardiologist find out, Doctor?"

"Ginger has a condition known as SAS, which stands for subaortic stenosis. The aortic valve separates the left ventricle, the heart's main pumping chamber, from the aorta, a large blood vessel that carries blood from the heart to the body. A stenosis is a blockage of the valve that keeps it from closing properly. The heart must then work harder to pump oxygen-laden blood into the body," explained the doctor.

"So what does that mean for Ginger?" asked Steve.

"Have you ever read stories about young basketball players who appear normal but suddenly fall over while running down a basketball court and then are pronounced dead?" he asked. "Like humans, dogs have a very high risk of sudden death with this condition."

I could see the concern growing on Steve's face as he asked, "What's the likelihood this can happen to Ginger?"

"I'm afraid the outlook is challenging," responded the veterinarian. "Eighty percent of dogs with Ginger's condition usually die by the time they are five years old."

I looked up at Steve and could see his eyes start to glisten. I tried to tell him with my eyes that everything would be fine and that he should not worry. Tears started rolling down his cheeks.

Trying to hold back his emotions, Steve asked, "What do we do from here?"

The doctor responded by saying, "Ginger should start taking a prescription drug called Atenolol, which is a generic brand of beta-blocker, a drug that controls the heart function to slow down the rate of beating and reduce stress on the heart. In Ginger's case this should extend her life. She also needs to control exercise but this is self-regulating because she will get tired and automatically slow down if she is exercising too hard."

Steve took me by my leash and thanked the veterinarian as we walked out of the examining room into the lobby. The look on the face of the receptionist suggested she also knew the bad news. It upset me knowing Steve's sadness. I could tell he was still fighting back tears as he lifted me into the back of the car for the drive home. Before he shut the door he cradled my head in his hands and, looking into my large brown eyes, said, "Ginger, you are going to be fine. If love can mend a broken heart, then you are going to be all right. We all love you that much."

Enter Max

The day after receiving such bad news, Steve called my breeder and told her of the discussion the previous day with my veterinarian and the findings of the canine cardiologist. She felt it impossible that one of her dogs could have such a life-threatening disease. Steve offered to fax her a copy of the report and she accepted.

After receiving and reviewing the report, she called Steve back the following day and apologized effusively for my condition and her reaction of disbelief. She wanted to know what she could do to help. She offered to take me back, which surprised me; I couldn't imagine leaving my new family now. Steve told her that giving me back after I had become such an important part of his family was out of the question. He knew Gabrielle would be devastated by such a decision. Next she offered another dog at no cost. Steve was silent for a moment. He considered how another dog could be a good backup plan. If something happened to me, Gabrielle would have bonded to the new dog, which would offset the loss. He told her yes. He would take another dog.

Steve decided he wanted a male this time and agreed with the breeder that he would receive the first male pick of her next available litter. I didn't like the sound of any of this. I had grown very comfortable in my new home, was now living most of my time outside of my crate, and enjoyed my role as beloved family pet. While I felt my heart condition was unfortunate, I trusted that I would be fine. I liked my new family and didn't want to share it with anyone else, human or canine. My role as cute adorable puppy was no longer assured.

The next available litter, born in October about a year and a half after I was born, included only one male along with six female puppies. The picking process was therefore unnecessary. Steve explained to Gabrielle that he wanted to have a second dog to keep me company. He suggested that I would be her dog and the new dog would be his to care for. Since Gabrielle was only ten years old, Steve decided against telling her of my condition. He didn't want her to be concerned and wanted her to fully enjoy the new arrival.

Steve decided on the name of Max for the new puppy. It was his deceased father's name and he felt Max was a great name for a male dog. I decided if I had to tolerate another dog in the house Max and Ginger had a nice ring to it. But I still wasn't enthused.

The day Max came home was wet and cold, a typical Pacific Northwest day in December. I got to ride along in the car with Steve and Gabrielle for the trip to the breeder's house. I enjoyed getting out of the car, racing around the yard, and meeting Max's parents. His father was an uncle of my father, making us cousins. Even though we were cousins, everyone referred to us as brother and sister.

One look at Max and I knew he was an older sister's worst nightmare. He was more than cute, he was adorable. His body was covered with soft downy fur and he had a large, handsome head and really big paws. I knew my days of being the center of attention at home were over. I would now have to share the limelight, a prospect I accepted reluctantly. But I relished being his older sister and getting to play with him.

Gabrielle

At the time Gabrielle picked me from my litter to join her life she was ten years old. As I got to know her, I felt she held some sadness that I didn't fully understand. Maybe it was a result of her parents' divorce. Moving back and forth between two houses every week was certainly not easy on her, and I expect she felt torn between two lives. After I arrived, her mother decided to get a dog of her own at Gabrielle's other home. I was a little jealous that she was spending time with another dog every other week, but when I found out it was a standard poodle I became more secure. Other than their rather tall and proud appearance and their tight, curly hair, which didn't shed, what was there to be jealous of? I mean, have you ever been around one? I didn't think they were very bright.

I remembered back to my parents' lessons about a dog's role with humans. I understood Gabrielle needed me and that it was my responsibility to let her know she was loved. Sneaking up into her bed at night was one of my favorite techniques. I'd sleep at her feet and keep her warm. I liked to slowly lick her hand in the morning when she woke up, and I continued to enjoy gazing into her beautiful blue eyes. Wherever Gab went around the house I would follow. I enjoyed the times she went down to the family room to watch a movie with friends. I could see she was happy, and it gave me a chance to curl up on the sofa and sleep, something I was very good at. I'm pretty sure my daily dose of Atenolol I was taking for my heart made me a bit drowsy, so a regular nap was just what I needed.

During these early years Gabrielle was very involved in competing with horses. She owned a horse named Coco, a champion Appaloosa. She rode in both western and English style but didn't perform jumping. She took lessons twice per week and during the spring and summers competed in horse shows in Washington and Oregon in cities such as Puyallup, Tacoma, Olympia, Ridgefield, and Boring.

The first time I ever saw a horse was my first trip out to the barn with Gabrielle. I found horses intimidating at first because they are so large and their big eyes frightened me. But I came to understand that even while big, they must not have a brain to match because they were always so skittish and afraid of me. I found I couldn't get very close to Coco because he would soon start kicking and straining at his halter. So I just watched Gabrielle groom, exercise, and ride Coco from a safe distance.

Max and I became regular attendees at the horse shows throughout the summers. Steve brought along a large portable metal fence he'd set up outside in nice weather or inside in a stall if it was raining. He always made sure we had a blanket to lie on and water to drink. I grew accustomed to watching everything and rarely slept.

I sensed that Gabrielle enjoyed time with the other girls on the team. Throughout the day they would help each other get dressed and their horses groomed for each event, borrowing brushes, halters, boot black, hair clips, and other necessities for competition. I was amazed that whenever Gabrielle was asked by a team mate to borrow a certain item, she knew exactly where to find it among all of the boxes and containers in her make-shift tack room assembled in a vacant horse stall. The girls cheered each other when they weren't in the same class and competed hard when they were. Their coach had always emphasized the importance of the team. Individual victories were a result of the success of the team and losses were an opportunity to work hard and improve.

For some of the events, Steve put on our leashes and walked Max and me to the arena to watch Gabrielle compete. I remember one specific day when Gabrielle was competing in an event called western equitation. She was required to ride her horse into the arena and then guide it through a pattern utilizing a series of gaits including walk, jog, and lope. Control, position on the horse, and mastery of the geometry of the pattern were all essential to winning high marks from the judges. From our position near the entrance to the arena we could see Gabrielle mount her horse and wait for her number to be called, indicating she could enter the arena. We then walked to a place to view the inside of the ring about thirty yards away.

As Gabrielle entered the arena for her first ride, she successfully navigated the course until about midway through. I thought she looked very stylish high upon her horse wearing a robin's egg blue jacket and pants with a tall white western hat. Suddenly I heard Steve say to a friend that she'd just gone off course by pivoting right instead of left for a 360-degree jog around the arena. This mistake was always grounds for immediate elimination. When Gabrielle rode out of the arena back to the practice area I saw she was in tears. She got off of her horse, and Steve and her coach both walked over just as she bent over and vomited on the arena dirt.

Her next event was the same western equitation pattern she had just completed but with a more senior class and would begin in a few minutes. I could hear Steve asking her if she wanted to scratch her name from the list of competitors and go lie down. She said no and told them she really wanted to do it. After a few sips of water and some quick words of encouragement from her coach, Gabrielle got back on Coco and waited again for her number to be called.

We walked back to our viewing spot next to the arena and I could tell from the look on Steve's face that he was as deeply concerned as I was. I looked over at Max and could see he was in complete disregard of the proceedings and instead was looking at the horses and other dogs and trying to run over to each human passing by. I wanted him to be more respectful, but Max was acting like a pretty normal dog.

Gabrielle's number was called and she entered the arena. Her ride through the pattern appeared to go flawlessly. When she arrived at the point where she needed to pivot left she did so without hesitation. She completed the pattern and rode out of the arena with a huge smile on her face. After all the competitors were finished and the scores were totaled Gabrielle had taken second place. It was a moment of emotional growth for her and marked a turning point. From that day forward she was more confident in her riding, suffered less anxiety, and never experienced an upset stomach again.

Shortly after that regional competition, she traveled to Oklahoma City for the National Appaloosa Show, a yearly event that brings in over one thousand horses and many more riders. She ended that ten-day event with one national championship in showmanship and a reserve placing in trail. She was a changed girl from then on and I was glad to have witnessed the transformation. Maybe that sadness I'd observed in her life was ebbing.

Gabrielle and her first golden retriever plush toy named Eddie.

Orange Girl and her litter mates shortly after birth.

Ginger tries to manage a tennis ball.

Gabrielle considers the puppies and wonders which one to choose.

Max and Ginger do what they do best.

Ginger caught sleeping with Gabrielle.

Gabrielle joins Ginger in her crate.

Max and Steve enjoy the beach on Bainbridge Island, Washington.

Max chases Ginger on Cannon Beach, Oregon.

Ginger enjoys a rare heavy winter snowstorm.

T. Mark Stover
3/18/1952 – 10/28/2009
Memory Eternal

Memorial program for Mark Stover.

Summer Camp for Dogs

Soon it was time for some puppy training. As required in the original purchase agreement, Steve and Gabrielle took me to an eight-week training course at a local canine behavior center. The class was full with fourteen puppies and their owners. Some puppies were young like me, others were older and in need of remedial training to correct behavior problems like barking, pulling on leashes, wandering out of a down and stay position, and generally just behaving like a normal dog. I think the real purpose of the training was to train the owners.

During the intervening week we went to parks or other open areas and practiced that week's lessons. At the end of the training, each dog was taken through a course by the owner demonstrating the ability of the dog to obey commands such as stand, sit, down, stay, come, and heel, both on and off leash. I completed the test with a score of 141 out of 165, easily passing the minimum score of 130. I was always a quick learner. In fact I knew that if I were a human going to school I'd be the class president, a straight A student, and the favorite of most teachers.

Max, on the other hand, was a very free spirit. He was always full of energy, was easily distracted, and jumped up at every opportunity while looking adorably cute. Steve decided on another training plan for him. From a neighbor he heard of a kennel and training facility on Kiket Island near Deception Pass in the northern Puget Sound area. Steve spoke with the owner, a man named Mark. He said he would be happy to take on the challenge of training Max and told Steve that once Max and I had all of our necessary lab tests and inoculations we could visit. In the following month Steve had planned a trip out of town so he scheduled our first visit to go meet Mark.

As we made the two-hour drive to the kennel, I was a little nervous since this would be the first time Max and I stayed away from our comfortable and familiar home. Near the island, Steve pulled off the main paved road onto a gravel road. He immediately stopped at a tall chain link fence with a large swinging gate. After passing through the gate, Steve continued down the drive toward the island.

Kiket Island is actually connected to Fidalgo Island by a narrow spit, so it's not technically a free-standing island. Kiket measures fifty-five acres in size and includes a large ranch-style house, an old tennis court, several out buildings, and many acres of beachfront all surrounded by old growth timber. As Max and I looked out the windows of the car while driving down the last hill toward the house we couldn't wait to get out and look around.

As Steve parked the car we were greeted by a young girl named Beth who welcomed Steve and said, "Let's see the kids."

Steve walked to the back of the car and put leashes on us before we jumped to the ground. Max bounced like a pogo stick jumping up and down on Beth who said, "Oh boy, we have some work to do."

Behind me I heard a very deep voice say, "Hello, Steve, this must be Max and Ginger."

I turned to see a man with a black mustache wearing aviator sunglasses and sporting a brown leather packer hat upon his head. He was dressed with a leather vest over a plaid shirt with thick wool pants on top of work boots. I was frightened by his deep voice and his unusual look. Max, as always, was just excited to meet a new person. As someone once said about golden retrievers, coming across a new human is another chance to make a friend.

Steve said, "Hello, Mark, it's a pleasure to meet you. Ginger here has been through puppy classes, but Max has never had any formal training, which I'm sure is quite obvious."

Mark responded that Max was a good-looking dog and that he'd take good care of us. He wanted to know where Steve was headed on vacation. Steve told him Palm Springs to visit his mother. That comment led to a long conversation about other clients who often traveled to Palm Springs. In the course of the conversation I learned that some of Mark's clients included dogs of a former governor, a former senator, one of the most highly paid athletes on the Seattle baseball franchise, and the CEO of a well-known local coffee company. We were suddenly among the dogs of Seattle's elite. Fortunately dogs don't care much about status. We just treat each other the same regardless of who our owners might be.

Beth took us by our leashes for a short walk before taking us to the kennel Max and I would share. Things seemed to be going well. That night after dinner, as it was getting dark, I saw Mark appear in the kennel building with a book under his arm. He no longer wore his dark sunglasses and seemed happy to see and hear us as we greeted him by barking and running around in our kennels. After saying hello to each dog by name, he sat down on a chair located under a bright light in the ceiling and opened his book. He read to us about American history, which was his favorite subject. We were quiet and respectful as he read and paid rapt attention. It was almost as if he were one of us. He was the first human I had met who could communicate with us so directly. I began to realize he was very different than other humans I had met. Over time I came to realize Mark was somewhat like Dr. Doolittle and George S. Patton all rolled into one.

The next day was the beginning of training for Max and several other dogs. I sat and watched as Beth tried to teach Max to sit and stay. I already knew how to do this so didn't need to participate. Beth had placed a number of old bath towels around the grassy training area. Her goal was to have each dog learn that once they were placed in a down position on the towel they were not to leave unless given the command of "done."

Max was a slow learner. He knew how to sit and lie down, but once Beth turned her focus to another dog, Max was quickly up and running wherever his nose led him. This went on a few times until I heard that familiar deep baritone voice say forcefully, "Max, get down and stay down."

Mark had quietly walked from the house onto the training yard and took control of the situation. Max quickly recognized that there would be no messing around if Mark was present and quickly got down and stayed. I was quite proud of him and the other dogs as I looked around and saw all six dogs lying down on their towels scattered haphazardly around the yard. Mark commanded incredible respect. He clearly knew how to talk to dogs.

The Middle Innings

As the years rolled by, I often thought how lucky I was that Gabrielle picked me. Steve was a great dog owner and gave us the best care. We ate healthy food twice per day, visited the veterinarian for routine care, and had access to a great emergency hospital nearby for care on weekends or late at night. We were normally walked twice per day including some time off leash at a nearby park where we would run and stay in shape. These walks occurred whether it was raining or dry, in daylight or at night. We were never overweight and Steve even cleaned our ears regularly, an important step to help golden retrievers avoid ear infections. Life was as good as it could get for an urban dog.

Gabrielle was growing up and continued to gain confidence in herself and her life. I couldn't help but notice that as she got older I became less of an interest for her. She had high school friends to spend time with and lots of homework. Gabrielle was a diligent student with great study habits fueled by a desire to stay on top of her work load. She still took me for walks, especially when reminded by Steve. But I understood that teenage girls are learning independence and at that age are often self-absorbed. This didn't change my feelings for her nor my dedication.

Steve and Max, on the other hand, were inseparable. I sometimes felt that Max was another child for Steve, maybe the son he never had. I know he loved Gabrielle as deeply as humanly possible, but he clearly enjoyed Max's company. They went on long runs or hikes together and even in the car to run around town and take care of errands. Due to my heart condition I couldn't run or hike like Max could, but Steve typically took me along in the car and gave me a walk before heading out with Max.

And it was clear Max adored Steve. If Steve left the house, Max would always wait by the door to the garage for him to return. When it was time to get up in the morning, Steve never really needed an alarm since Max was usually there with his paws up on the bed wanting to be rubbed and for Steve to get out of bed and go downstairs and feed him breakfast. I used to watch this every morning curled up in my bed on the floor in Steve's bedroom with one eye open wondering where Max got his enthusiasm. I don't think I ever saw him get tired.

When Steve took him hiking, Max usually received about three times the exercise Steve did because he was always running up ahead on the trail out of sight, then back down to make sure Steve was still there, then back up the trail, and so on for the duration of the hike. If later in the day Steve wanted to go run or walk again, Max was always up for it. They were great pals.

During this time I continued to see my canine cardiologist on a yearly basis for an ultrasound assessment of the condition of my heart. It never worsened but didn't improve either. On my fifth year of these visits, Steve and the veterinarian were ecstatic that I had beaten the odds. I had survived the disease, which typically kills 80 percent of dogs with my condition in five years, and I was now less likely to suffer a sudden death. A remaining concern was a possible lung or heart infection possibly caused by contaminated blood back flowing into my heart. By continuing to take the beta blocker and receiving regular exercise I was expected to lead a normal life.

When Steve was out of town, we continued to stay with Mark up at Kiket Island. Sometimes he would pick us up at home in a large white cargo van filled with many crates and dogs inside for the ride up to the island. Max and I enjoyed those trips, especially those nights he would come into the kennel and read to us before going to bed. His German shepherd named Ding was always at his side on those nights and lay at his feet while he read.

There were many dogs that arrived at the kennel that seemed untreatable. Their owners had tried everything and were ready to give up until learning of Mark and his abilities. Mark worked with their dogs as long as necessary until a new sense of calm and obedience was established. Even Max was a different dog around Mark. Wherever he was when Mark appeared, whether in the kennel, out on the grass training area, or at home, Max quickly sat down with his head erect and eyes straight ahead as if he was in the army and Mark was his drill sergeant. Mark was one of those rare humans my parents told us about who understood and could communicate with dogs. "There were few in the world," they said, "but when we came across one it was obvious." Mark was one of them.

My life was great and I was very content during these years. I had a great family. I lived in a comfortable home with a fenced back yard. Gabrielle was a sweet girl whom I was watching grow into a beautiful and confident young woman. Although Max wasn't the brightest dog on the block, his enthusiastic disposition and his handsome good looks made him a great brother. We had fun times swimming together, sharing toys, sleeping side by side, and trusting one another completely. I was a very lucky dog indeed.

Humans Disappoint

One fall evening when I was six years old, Steve received a phone call at home from a friend of his, Sharon, who had a lovable yellow lab named Charlie. Charlie was also a frequent guest of Mark's kennel. Mark often came to Sharon's home to help train Charlie and Sharon's daughter with obedience techniques. Sharon's call was of an urgent nature; she wanted to know if Steve had heard the upsetting news about Mark. She told him to turn on the television and watch the news. She was in tears as she quickly hung up.

Steve listened to the news and was instantly affected. I could tell by the look on his face and its loss of color. The news anchor said that Mark had been reported missing a few days earlier and sheriff's deputies investigating his house that morning had found his dog Ding seriously injured with a gunshot to his face but alive. Blood was smeared on the walls inside the home. These authorities feared that Mark had been murdered. I couldn't believe it. Why would anyone want to harm Mark or Ding?

Through some good fortune and the sharp eyes of someone driving by in a car early in the morning of Mark's disappearance, a car was spotted and determined to belong to the boyfriend of Mark's ex-wife. A county sheriff's officer quickly tracked him down to the ex-wife's home in eastern Washington. When he arrived at the home to arrest the suspect, the suspect was observed to throw a plastic bag down into a nearby ravine. The bag was later examined and found to contain a gun. Lab tests linked the gun to some bullet cases found at Mark's home, and the gun was similar to the model of gun used to shoot Ding. Since Mark's body has yet to be recovered, it's not possible to know if it was the same gun used to shoot him, if that is what happened.

The public's support of Mark was instantaneous and far reaching. A web site was established for people to write about the wonderful contributions Mark had made to their lives and the lives of their dogs. Cited in the press as the "Dog Whisperer of Seattle" with an elite client list, it was not surprising to see the outpouring of concern for Mark and Ding.

Steve went to the Skagit County courthouse a few times to attend hearings and read through the case docket. On his first visit, shortly after the arrest, Steve took Max and me to go visit the kennel. The property was cordoned off with police tape and barricades preventing us from driving up the road, but we were able to walk up near the exercise area. There on the chain link fence many mourners had placed flowers and photos of their dogs, creating a collage of images. I noticed tears welling up in Steve's eyes as he looked at the photos and gazed up at the fenced play area where he had watched Max and me receiving training and playing over the years. Our last stay had only been a few months earlier.

Steve mourned the loss of Mark. Having taken great comfort knowing we were in Mark's safe hands while he was out of town, Steve knew it would be hard to ever find another person he trusted to take care of us. He had also considered Mark a friend and valued their relationship tremendously. During the trial, which spanned almost four weeks, Steve either watched the proceedings live on his computer or late into the evening with a recording of the day's testimony. As I sat on the floor in his office I often saw photos of Ding and Mark on the computer screen.

As Steve and I watched the court clerk announce the verdict of the jury, I noticed the children sitting behind their father who had been accused of Mark's murder. Upon hearing the phrase "guilty in the first degree..." the three children immediately broke into tears, sobbing and kicking the bench as they were overcome with grief. Not only had their father robbed the Seattle area of a uniquely gifted dog trainer, he had also taken himself out of their lives and would soon be spending many years in prison. Who would now take care of them I wondered. It made me sad and angry.

Time to Go

Soon after Mark's death, Gabrielle was preparing to graduate from high school and go to college. I'm not sure what people do in college; maybe it's like obedience school but for humans. Gabrielle said students study and take tests just as I did when I went to obedience school. I knew she would be too busy to take care of me at college and I would not be going along. Gabrielle was excited to be leaving the Pacific Northwest for California with its sunnier weather and distance from her parents.

Shortly after she left, I started to have problems with my heart. It happened one day when I was running off leash in the park with Max. I suddenly became very tired and fell over. As I lay on the grass gasping for breath with my heart racing I feared something terrible was happening. Steve rushed over, scooped me up in his hands, and carried me over to the car, commanding Max to follow. We drove to the animal hospital where I was seen immediately while Steve waited in the reception area and Max waited in the car. I was given an injection and soon felt better.

When Steve was escorted back to join me in the examination room, the veterinarian told him that I had suffered a minor stroke from low blood flow failing to carry enough oxygen to my brain. He said it wasn't good news and that Steve would have to watch me carefully.

I felt very tired the next day and a little better the following day. But I never regained the strength I'd had that day running in the park. A week later I grew very tired. Not tired as when I was running, but all I wanted to do was sleep. I wasn't hungry and didn't eat my meals. I could see the worried look on Steve's face, which naturally caused me concern. He decided to take me to see the veterinarian again. I couldn't hear the conversation the doctor had with Steve after my examination, but it couldn't have been very good because when Steve came in to pick me up tears were running down his cheeks and he couldn't talk. He just looked at me with his big blue eyes.

The rest of that evening at home he often hugged me and told me how much he loved me. I realized that this was the time my parents had told me would someday arrive. It was the time when I would leave my family after my assignment was complete. Reflecting upon my life, I felt I had tried my best to live up to the lessons of my parents. I loved Gabrielle and hope I had successfully taught her how important it is to care for all living things. I hoped she had learned compassion and responsibility and would be better prepared to love other humans unconditionally. For that is what dogs do. We wait by the door for our humans to come home no matter how long they have been gone or where they have traveled.

The following morning was my last in Steve's home. He took me to the veterinarian's office where the doctor asked Steve to join me in the examination room. The doctor explained to Steve that this was the best course of action, that my heart was infected and it was better to let my life end this way than suffer from pain and a deteriorating life at home. Steve just stood there nodding and crying and tried his best to blurt out, "I understand."

I think I understood what was about to happen. And I couldn't help but feel there was a link between Gabrielle growing up and leaving home for college with what was about to happen to me and where I might be going. It was as if we both were moving on to begin another phase of life after successfully completing the preceding phase. There was definitely some symmetry about it.

The doctor shaved my upper right front leg until it was clean of fur and showed only bright pink skin. After cleaning the area with disinfectant, he applied topical Lidocaine to deaden the area. He opened a catheter and slowly inserted the needle into my leg and taped it into place. He then told Steve that I would just go to sleep and wouldn't feel any discomfort. I could see that tears were still streaming down Steve's face. I stared at him and tried my best to communicate with my eyes these thoughts:

Steve, I love you as I know you have loved me. You have been the best owner a dog could ever hope for. Your daughter Gabrielle is a very sweet girl who is going to have a great life. I have tried my best to love her and teach her the value of caring for others. I know she has sadness in her life but I hope I have brought her some joy. Tell Max he was the best brother, even if he could be most obnoxious. I'll miss him too, but I'm glad to know he will still be watching over you and teaching you about love in his own way.

The doctor then looked at me and said, "Good-bye, Ginger. Everyone here in the office thinks you are the most amazing dog we've ever served." Next he attached a syringe filled with liquid to the tube leading out of the catheter. And then he gave me a wink. I almost didn't notice it. It was the glorious sign my parents had told me to watch for. The sign that reassured me everything would be all right. He slowly pressed the plunger and I fell asleep.

Reborn

The next thing I remember was the hum of tires on pavement. I opened my eyes and couldn't quite comprehend what I was seeing. I was inside the same van that used to take us up to Kiket Island. Several other dogs were with me in the van in separate kennels. I looked down at my paw, and the shaved area was still there as was the mark from the catheter. So my experience in the veterinary office wasn't a dream.

After some amount of time, I heard the tires rolling on gravel and then the van stopped. The driver got out of the van and I could hear him open a gate so we could drive through. After closing it again we started driving down a gravel road. This all seemed very familiar but yet still foreign. I felt sleepy.

After a few more minutes the van stopped and the side door opened. As the sun streamed in I heard a voice I never expected to hear again, that low and deep, raspy voice say, "Hello, Queenie, how are you this fine day?" It was Mark. But he was dead, and I was pretty sure I was supposed to be dead. What was going on?

As he put me on a leash and got me out of the crate, he and his assistant Beth gathered all of the dogs around and told us they had some things to explain. I looked over and was surprised to see Ding, Mark's German shepherd, sitting next to us too. We all sat down on the same grassy area where we had received training and listened motionlessly as Mark began to speak.

"When you were young puppies and ready to go to your families, your parents told you about your responsibilities as dogs. They told you how your role in life was to add to the experience of humans, to help them lead richer, fuller, and more responsible lives though the love of a dog. What they didn't tell you, and what I didn't know until recently, is that when it was time for you to leave your families, you wouldn't actually die. Instead, you would come here. This place is a refuge for dogs and, as you noticed, looks a lot like the kennel where you came to stay and learn from me. When I disappeared I had the same good fortune to return here. I guess I must be an honorary dog given my past experiences with you. But here on this island, a place where humans can't visit, we have a new set of responsibilities.

"You will become teachers, just as your parents taught you. You will go back to a breeder and will be assigned a new litter of puppies to train. Once they have been assigned to their families, you will come back here and enjoy the rest of your lives as you see fit. You can go swim at the beach. Or go hike in the woods and find some squirrels to chase. Or you can come back here and play with your friends. It's all up to you. But every night after dinner when it's time for lights out, Ding and I will come down and I will read you more stories about American history. It's great to have you back, Ginger."

The joy I felt was immeasurable. I looked forward to having my own puppies and sharing my knowledge with them. I never expected to see Mark again and was reassured to be in his presence. I was also excited to go find my parents who were here. But best of all was realizing the day would come when Max would arrive and join me here. And he would tell me all about the rest of his life with Steve and Gabrielle.

Author's Note

As I conceived this memoir, I started out wanting to tell a story about my daughter and the pride I've felt watching her grow and mature into the young lady she is today. An important part of our lives together has been the addition of our two dogs to our family. From there I developed the idea of a personal memoir told through the eyes of Ginger, our first golden retriever.

Although based on true events that have occurred over the years, the book is obviously a work of fiction. My hope is to capture the loving personality of our dogs while at the same time express thankfulness for the dimension they add to our human lives. I hope I have succeeded. Ginger is a wise dog who understands human needs to a degree that at times seems uncanny.

I also tried to express my deep appreciation for the friendship I felt toward noted dog trainer Mark Stover who spent many hours with both dogs. His murder affected me profoundly and I will feel his loss the rest of my life. I watched every hour of testimony throughout the three-week trial, which ended in October, and was gratified that justice prevailed and his murderer was found guilty. He was a man who could truly talk with dogs. I will never forget the gift of love he gave them.

Author Information

Steven Wells is a writer living in Medina, Washington. After a career in high technology, he studied non-fiction writing at the University of Washington and published his first short story in the *Seattle Post Intelligencer*. He has also published several travel articles. *Ginger's Story* is his first book.

While not spending time with his dogs and daughter, Steve is also an aspiring wine maker and spends most harvests with local wineries helping to coax grapes into the bottle. He enjoys most outdoor activities including running, hiking, skiing, and bicycling.

Made in the USA
Charleston, SC
29 November 2011